MORE

I'M THROUGH! WHAT CAN I DO?

Editor: Stacey Faulkner
Cover Illustrator: Karl Edwards
Cover Designer: Barbara Peterson
Designer/Production: Alicia Schulte
Art Director: Moonhee Pak
Project Director: Betsy Morris, PhD

Table of Contents

Introduction

More I'm Through! What Can I Do? is a one-stop resource that addresses this all-too-familiar question teachers hear from students who finish early. The high-interest, ready-to-use puzzles, riddles, brainteasers, and mazes can be completed with minimal teacher assistance and help sharpen language arts, math, creative thinking, and critical thinking skills. This new series is a follow-up to our best-selling titles *I'm Through! What Can I Do?*

GETTING STARTED

Use any of the following suggestions to create a simple, structured environment that allows students to access these activities independently and keeps busy classrooms running smoothly.

1. Create individual student packets using all of the activity pages. Have students keep the packets in their desks and complete pages if they finish their assigned work early.

2. Create smaller packets by content areas (language arts and math) to use at centers. Store each set of packets in a file folder. Attach a class list to the outside of each folder. Have students cross out their names after they complete the packet.

3. Use activity pages individually as
   - supplements to specific lessons
   - homework assignments
   - substitute teacher's helpers
   - three-minute transition activities
   - morning warm-up or after-lunch refocusing activities

HELPFUL TIPS TO FREE YOUR TIME
   - Allow students to consult classmates to figure out puzzles.
   - Encourage students to correct each other's work.
   - Place copies of the answer key in an accessible area for students to pull as needed for self-correction.
   - Give students copies of the Student Recording Sheet (page 4) to keep track of completed activity pages. Have students color in or check off each activity after it is completed.

However you choose to use the activity pages, let *More I'm Through! What Can I Do?* assist you in establishing a constructive and productive classroom environment.

Name: _____

Keep track of your work by filling in the box after completing the activity.

p. 5	p. 6	p. 7	p. 8	p. 9	p. 10	p. 11	p. 12	p. 13	p. 14
p. 15	p. 16	p. 17	p. 18	p. 19	p. 20	p. 21	p. 22	p. 23	p. 24
p. 25	p. 26	p. 27	p. 28	p. 29	p. 30	p. 31	p. 32	p. 33	p. 34
p. 35	p. 36	p. 37	p. 38	p. 39	p. 40	p. 41	p. 42	p. 43	p. 44
p. 45	p. 46	p. 47	p. 48	p. 49	p. 50	p. 51	p. 52	p. 53	p. 54
p. 55	p. 56	p. 57	p. 58	p. 59	p. 60	p. 61	p. 62	p. 63	p. 64
p. 65	p. 66	p. 67	p. 68	p. 69	p. 70	p. 71	p. 72	p. 73	p. 74
p. 75	p. 76	p. 77	p. 78	p. 79	p. 80	p. 81	p. 82	p. 83	p. 84
p. 85	p. 86	p. 87	p. 88	p. 89	p. 90	p. 91			

Three-in-a-Row—Long O

Read the word in each box. Draw a line through three **long o** words in a row. Lines can go across, up and down, or on a slant. There may be more than one solution. Score one point for each set you find.

drop	pocket	zero
pop	coat	echo
road	got	tone

boat	tote	copy
rock	row	pot
rod	moat	toe

hope	knock	cot
hello	bowl	body
rose	globe	bone

zoom	odd	auto
oat	note	roll
mow	bomb	boa

Score: _____

Three-in-a-Row—2-Syllable Words

Read the word in each box. Draw a line through three **2-syllable** words in a row. Lines can go across, up and down, or on a slant. There may be more than one solution. Score one point for each set you find.

about	little	zero
copy	rock	thing
apple	how	play

have	echo	bear
went	happy	coat
into	after	lion

pocket	road	best
jump	city	crash
also	again	other

drink	odd	name
first	knew	school
many	people	bottom

Score: _____

More I'm Through! What Can I Do? Grade 2 © 2008 Creative Teaching Press

Three-in-a-Row—Nouns

Read the word in each box. Draw a line through three **noun** words in a row. Lines can go across, up and down, or on a slant. There may be more than one solution. Score one point for each set you find.

blow	river	clock
yellow	coat	cry
school	dirt	move

nose	rain	grass
quiet	tell	blue
math	head	horse

shoe	hope	game
clap	jeep	flag
best	flat	egg

horn	kind	run
name	hand	crab
mask	glad	sleep

Score:_____

Find the Rhyme #1

Say the name of each picture. If the name rhymes with the word written below it, color the picture.

sprain	trace	hair
bread	lake	pen
pale	cold	rail
brave	cape	swim

On the back of your paper, write the rhyming pairs you found.

More I'm Through! What Can I Do? Grade 2 © 2008 Creative Teaching Press

Name: _____ Date: _____

Find the Rhyme #2

Read each clue.
Write the correct rhyming word.

1. It begins with **/sw/** and rhymes with **meet**.

What is the word? _____

2. It begins with **/tr/** and rhymes with **rain**.

What is the word? _____

3. It begins with **/gl/** and rhymes with **robe**.

What is the word? _____

4. It begins with **/spr/** and rhymes with **ring**.

What is the word? _____

5. It begins with **/sn/** and rhymes with **lake**.

What is the word? _____

6. It begins with **/fl/** and rhymes with **rash**.

What is the word? _____

7. It begins with **/fr/** and rhymes with **log**.

What is the word? _____

8. It begins with **/thr/** and rhymes with **blow**.

What is the word? _____

9. It begins with **/cr/** and rhymes with **fly**.

What is the word? _____

10. It begins with **/str/** and rhymes with **fetch**.

What is the word? _____

Name: _____   Date: _____

Find the Hidden Picture—
Hard and Soft *c* and *g*

Read the words in the spaces. Follow the color key below.

Green—**hard *c*** words   Yellow—**hard *g*** words

Blue—**soft *c*** words   Red—**soft *g*** words

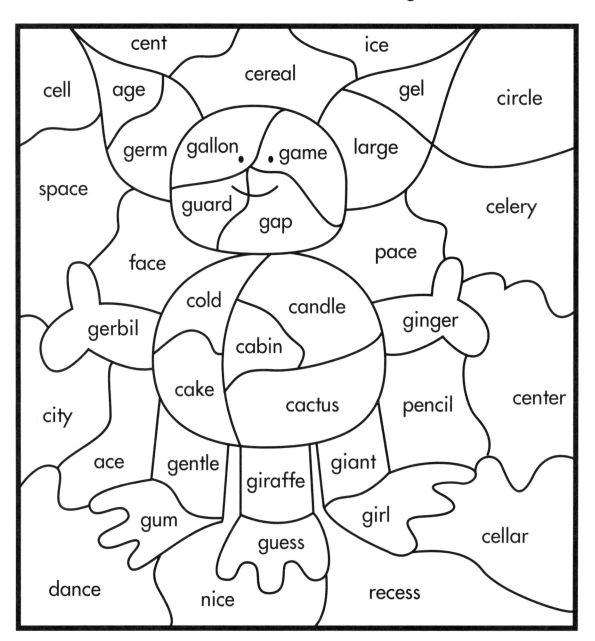

I see _____.

More I'm Through! What Can I Do? Grade 2 © 2008 Creative Teaching Press

Name: _____ Date: _____

Find the Hidden Picture—
How Many Syllables?

Read the words in the spaces. Follow the color key below.

Blue—**1-syllable** words Green—**2-syllable** words Brown—**3-syllable** words

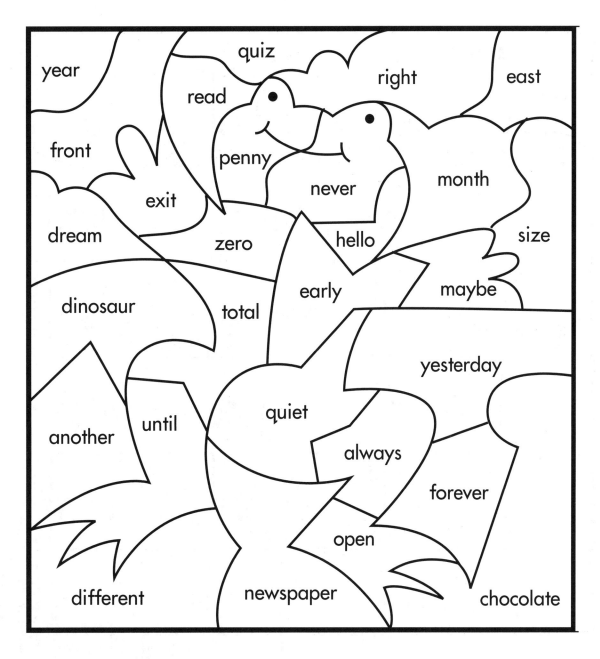

I see _____.

More I'm Through! What Can I Do? Grade 2 © 2008 Creative Teaching Press

Find Your Way—Words with *str*

Help the bus get to the school. Add **str** in front of the letters in each box.
Color the boxes that have real words to make a path.

eet	ike	an
ime	ing	ice
ed	eam	ish
ame	ipe	ap
eed	en	ain

Find Your Way—ABC Order

Help the dog get to the bone. Look at the beginning letter(s) of each word. Color the boxes in ABC order to make a path.

again	because	bath
first	boat	help
gave	grip	kind
goes	made	mine
open	most	pull

Find Your Way—Action Words

Help the grasshopper hop to the leaf. Color the boxes with action words to make a path.

skip	boat	pretty
look	swim	top
nice	buy	tree
pen	jump	give
dime	oven	sing

More I'm Through! What Can I Do? Grade 2 © 2008 Creative Teaching Press

Word Builder—Friend

Look at the word. Use the letters to make other words.

FRIEND

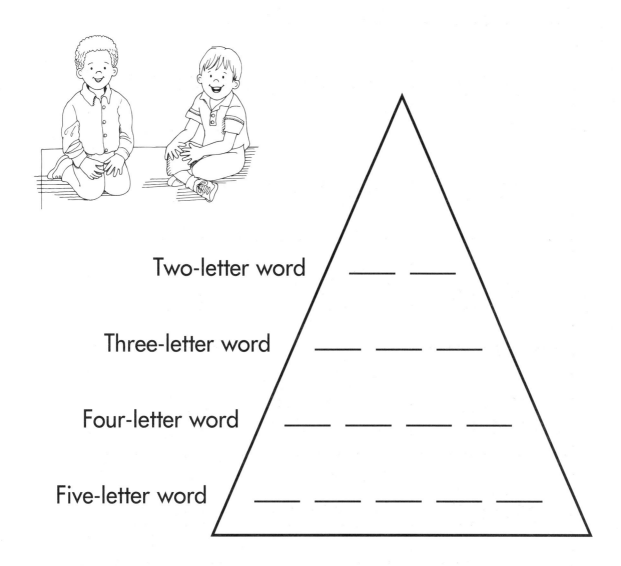

Two-letter word   __ __

Three-letter word   __ __ __

Four-letter word   __ __ __ __

Five-letter word   __ __ __ __ __

On the back of your paper, make a list of other words you can build.

Name: _____   Date: _____

Word Builder—Birthday

Look at the word. Use the letters to make other words.

BIRTHDAY

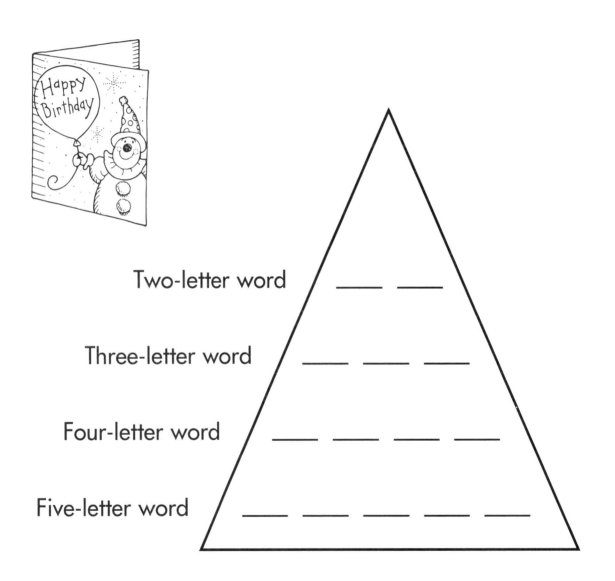

Two-letter word   ___ ___

Three-letter word   ___ ___ ___

Four-letter word   ___ ___ ___ ___

Five-letter word   ___ ___ ___ ___ ___

On the back of your paper, make a list of other words you can build.

More I'm Through! What Can I Do? Grade 2 © 2008 Creative Teaching Press

Word Builder—Racetrack

Look at the word. Use the letters to make other words.

RACETRACK

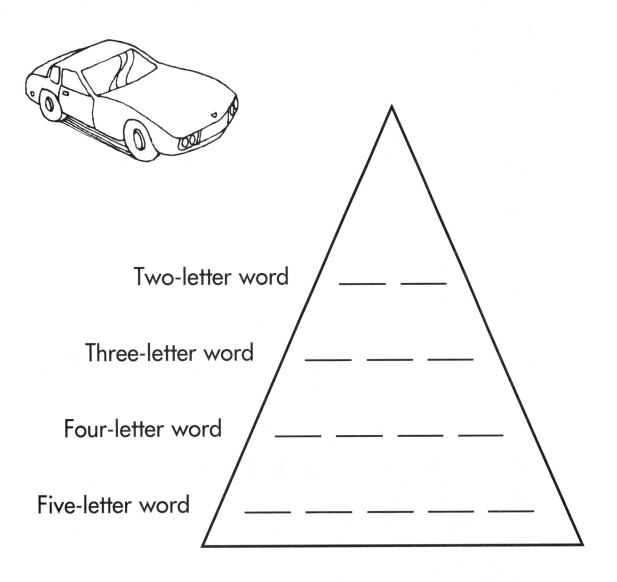

Two-letter word   ___ ___

Three-letter word   ___ ___ ___

Four-letter word   ___ ___ ___ ___

Five-letter word   ___ ___ ___ ___ ___

On the back of your paper, make a list of other words you can build.

Word Scramble—
Mystery Long e Sound

The letters in these words are all mixed up. Put the letters in order to make **long e** words. Copy the letters with numbers underneath to the matching numbers below to solve the riddle.

1. nkee ___ ___ ___ ___
　　　　　　　 11

2. terta ___ ___ ___ ___ ___
　　　　　　 15　　　　 6

3. heewl ___ ___ ___ ___ ___
　　　　　　 2　　　　 10

4. reetts ___ ___ ___ ___ ___
　　　　 5　 13

5. sephe ___ ___ ___ ___ ___
　　　　　　　 3

6. swete ___ ___ ___ ___ ___
　　　　　 17　　　　　　　 1

7. tyci ___ ___ ___ ___
　　　　　 16　 12　 4

8. emet ___ ___ ___ ___
　　　　　　 7

9. bayb ___ ___ ___ ___
　　　　　　　　　 9

10. rela ___ ___ ___ ___
　　　　 8　 14

What mystery letter copies the **long e** sound?

　　　　　　　　　　 m
___ ___ ___ ___ ___ ___ ___ ___ ___
 1　 2　 3　　　 4　 5　 6　 7　 8　 9

___ ___ ___ ___ ___ ___ ___ ___ ___ !
 10　 11　 12　 13　 14　 15　 16　 17　 4

More I'm Through! What Can I Do? Grade 2 © 2008 Creative Teaching Press

Word Scramble—*R*-Controlled Vowels

The letters in these words are all mixed up. Put the letters in order to make **r-controlled vowel** words. Copy the letters with numbers underneath to the matching numbers below to solve the riddle.

1. trid ___ ___ ___ ___
                          1

2. trsif ___ ___ ___ ___ ___
                              6

3. norh ___ ___ ___ ___
                    10

4. letutr ___ ___ ___ ___ ___ ___
                              4   8

5. fiengr ___ ___ ___ ___ ___ ___
                                  5

6. drta ___ ___ ___ ___
                          7

7. reh ___ ___ ___
                3

8. arc ___ ___ ___

9. ruht ___ ___ ___ ___
                2

10. rbdi ___ ___ ___ ___
                          9

What it is in the middle of Paris?

___ ___ ___   ___ ___ ___ ___ ___ ___   ___ !
 1   2   3   4   5   6   7   8   9   10

Word Scramble—Fruits and Vegetables

The letters in these words are all mixed up. Put the letters in order to make words that name fruits or vegetables. Copy the letters with numbers underneath to the matching numbers below to solve the riddle.

1. noager ___ ___ ___ ___ ___ ___
                        4

2. nabnaa ___ ___ ___ ___ ___ ___

3. aesbn ___ ___ ___ ___ ___
                  10

4. plpae ___ ___ ___ ___ ___
                      6   15

5. raishd ___ ___ ___ ___ ___ ___
                       2

6. looricbc ___ ___ ___ ___ ___ ___ ___ ___
                                          3   9

7. wiik ___ ___ ___ ___
                  1   13

8. ctrrao ___ ___ ___ ___ ___ ___
                           11   5

9. reecly ___ ___ ___ ___ ___ ___
                      7   16   14   12

10. parseg ___ ___ ___ ___ ___ ___
                                 8

What did the baby banana say to its father?

___ ___ ___ ___ ___   ___ ___ ___ ___
 1   2   3   4   5   6   7   8   9

___ ___ ___ ___   ___ ___ ___ ___ .
 V 10 11 12   13 14 15 16

More I'm Through! What Can I Do? Grade 2 © 2008 Creative Teaching Press

Magic Word Square #1

How many words can you find in the square? Start on any square and move one square at a time in any direction. You may not skip a square. Write the words you find on the lines.

B	H	W
M	O	P
Y	L	S

Words I Found:

_____hop_____   _____   _____

_____   _____   _____

_____   _____   _____

_____   _____   _____

More I'm Through! What Can I Do? Grade 2 © 2008 Creative Teaching Press

Magic Word Square #2

How many words can you find in the square? Start on any square and move one square at a time in any direction. You may not skip a square. Write the words you find on the lines.

E	L	N
O	Y	A
N	L	P

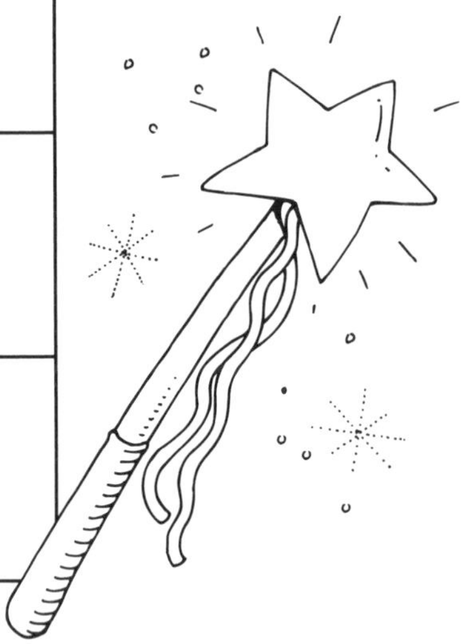

Words I Found:

_____ any _____   _____

_____   _____   _____

_____   _____   _____

_____   _____   _____

_____   _____   _____

More I'm Through! What Can I Do? Grade 2 © 2008 Creative Teaching Press

Compound Crossword

Read each clue. Each answer forms a compound word. Write each word in the puzzle.

Across

1. What ants build.

2. A type of fly that is very large.

5. An ocean animal with five arms.

6. What you boil tea in.

7. What a baby plays in.

Down

1. What you take to fly across the country.

3. What lights the shore at night for ships at sea.

4. A popular summertime sport.

Same or Opposite? Crossword

Read each clue. Each answer is a synonym or antonym of the clue. Write each word in the puzzle.

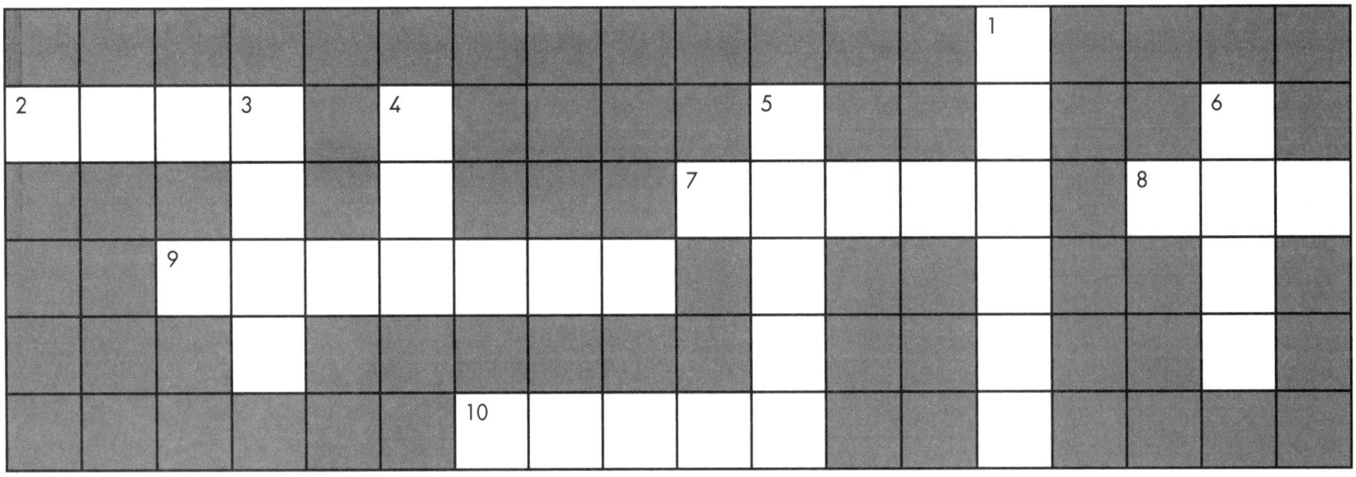

Across

2. opposite of cruel

7. opposite of last

8. to purchase

9. to copy

10. opposite of sour

Down

1. to collect

3. a little wet

4. opposite of cold

5. not heavy

6. opposite of empty

Word Bank		
buy	gather	light
damp	hot	sweet
first	imitate	
full	kind	

Human Body Word Search

Look at the words in the box. Find and circle the words hidden in the puzzle. Words can be found left to right, top to bottom, and backwards.

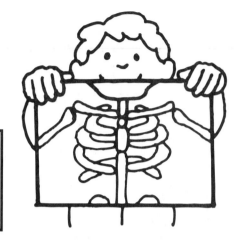

BONES	ELBOW	LUNGS	STOMACH
BRAIN	HEART	MUSCLES	DIGESTION
JOINTS	NERVES		

```
J  R  Y  V  V  X  U  H  L  S
E  L  L  J  D  W  N  E  U  E
E  A  Q  A  L  U  Q  A  N  L
S  T  O  M  A  C  H  R  G  C
N  T  U  F  H  G  G  T  S  S
D  I  G  E  S  T  I  O  N  U
I  T  S  R  E  L  B  O  W  M
A  J  O  I  N  T  S  J  N  Q
S  E  V  R  E  N  C  H  C  V
B  R  A  I  N  S  E  N  O  B
```

Name: _____   Date: _____

Types of Animals Word Search

Look at the words in the box. Find and circle the words hidden in the puzzle. Words can be found left to right, top to bottom, and on a slant.

BEAR	HORSE	PARROT	SNAKE
CARDINAL	LIZARD	SALAMANDER	TIGER
CLOWNFISH	NEWT	SHARK	TOAD

```
T  I  G  E  R  Z  N  J  G  R  P  T
V  E  A  T  I  D  A  T  E  S  W  O
C  I  H  Z  W  C  C  D  L  M  X  A
D  A  C  L  O  W  N  F  I  S  H  D
H  T  R  B  E  A  R  N  M  D  H  T
D  O  S  D  M  S  A  V  P  S  H  F
N  N  R  A  I  R  P  E  A  H  Q  E
R  E  L  S  D  N  K  G  R  A  S  I
E  A  W  U  E  A  A  A  R  R  S  K
S  F  R  T  N  P  V  L  O  K  G  A
G  S  Y  S  W  B  O  D  T  P  L  E
F  Q  N  O  K  J  L  I  Z  A  R  D
```

More I'm Through! What Can I Do? Grade 2 © 2008 Creative Teaching Press

Landforms and Bodies of Water Word Search

Look at the words in the box. Find and circle the words hidden in the puzzle. Words can be found left to right, top to bottom, and on a slant.

BAY	LAKE	OCEAN	POND
HILL	MESA	PENINSULA	RIVER
ISLAND	MOUNTAIN	PLAIN	VALLEY

```
F  B  H  C  D  P  L  A  I  N  V  V
V  J  A  G  F  E  V  G  W  P  A  Z
L  L  V  Y  S  N  T  N  P  R  L  A
D  A  N  T  T  I  W  N  K  E  L  U
F  C  K  I  I  N  U  M  W  O  E  N
V  I  N  E  D  S  L  V  Y  J  Y  N
R  Z  S  Q  X  U  S  E  L  P  A  V
I  X  D  L  N  L  Y  B  L  E  P  J
V  H  Z  T  A  A  P  L  C  Z  O  A
E  M  A  K  Z  N  I  O  Y  T  N  S
R  I  X  S  J  H  D  Q  Y  N  D  M
M  E  S  A  M  O  U  N  T  A  I  N
```

Fun with Words #1

Complete the chart. Write words that begin with each letter.

	g	r	o	w
Fruit				
Animal				
Place				
Name				

Fun with Words #2

For each category write a word that begins with the letter on the left. Score one point for each word. Earn five bonus points for any category where you have no incorrect answers or blanks.

Letter	One-Syllable Words (boat)	Two-Syllable Words (baby)	Nouns (book)	Compound Words (butterfly)	Score
A					
C					
M					
O					
W					
				Total	
				Bonus	
				Final Score	

The Five Senses

Using your five senses helps you think of descriptive words. Read the words on each snake. Color in the sections that contain describing words that match the sense on the snake's cap.

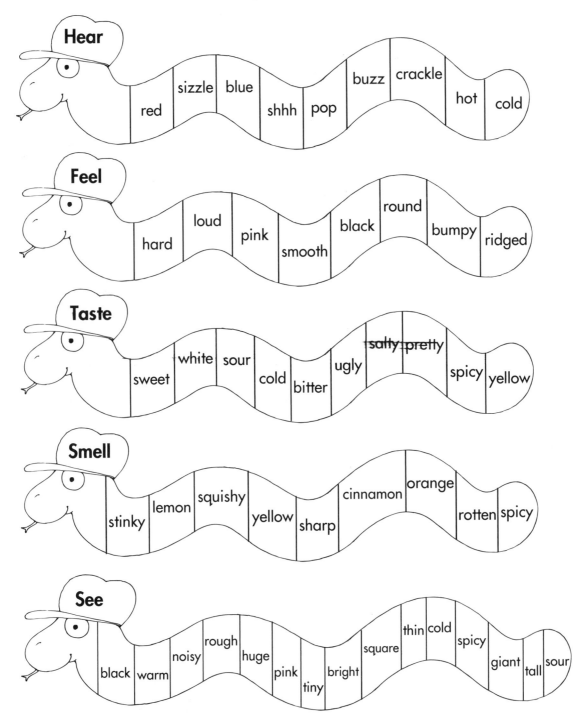

Hear
red | sizzle | blue | shhh | pop | buzz | crackle | hot | cold

Feel
hard | loud | pink | smooth | black | round | bumpy | ridged

Taste
sweet | white | sour | cold | bitter | ugly | salty | pretty | spicy | yellow

Smell
stinky | lemon | squishy | yellow | sharp | cinnamon | orange | rotten | spicy

See
black | warm | noisy | rough | huge | pink | tiny | bright | square | thin | cold | spicy | giant | tall | sour

More I'm Through! What Can I Do? Grade 2 © 2008 Creative Teaching Press

Adding Details

Use the secret code to add words that tell where, when, why, or how about each subject and verb.

1. The snake slithered

_____
A ●

_____
B ■

_____
E ▲

_____ .
C ▲

2. The patient waited

_____
B ●

_____
A ■

_____ .
B ▲

3. The dog played

_____
C ●

_____
B ■

_____ .
C ■

4. She showed up

_____
B ★

_____
B ●

_____ .
C ★

5. A friend called

_____
D ●

_____   _____ .
A ▲   D ■

6. The boy swam

_____
D ▲

_____
E ■

_____
E ★

_____ .
A ★

	●	■	▲	★
A	along	her	after	lake
B	for	the	doctor	late
C	in	yard	path	work
D	yesterday	school	in	south
E	winter	the	rocky	cold

More I'm Through! What Can I Do? Grade 2 © 2008 Creative Teaching Press

Main Idea and Details— All About Families

Color in the children who are sharing a detail that supports the main idea.

Main Idea: | I love to spend time with my family.

My family eats meals together.

Ms. Morris is a great gym teacher.

My mom and I enjoy playing games.

I have a dentist appointment on Friday.

My sister and I ride bikes after school.

I like to bring my own lunch to school.

After dinner we help each other clean up.

I got an A on my spelling test.

What's the Main Idea?

For each set of items listed below, write the main idea that best represents it.

1.

apple

banana

lemon

grapes

watermelon

_____

2.

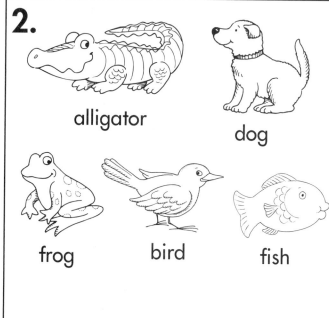

alligator

dog

frog

bird

fish

_____

3.

happy

mad

tired

sad

_____

4.

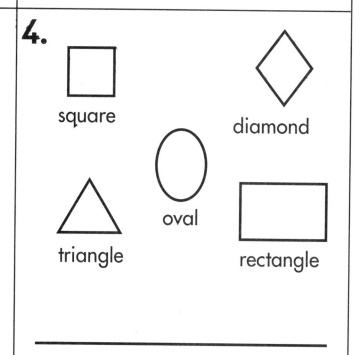

square

diamond

triangle

oval

rectangle

_____

Name: _____   Date: _____

Main Idea and Details—
A Day of Fun

Fill in each box with some details about what you can do at each location.

1.

The Beach

_____

_____

_____

2.

The Park

_____

_____

_____

3.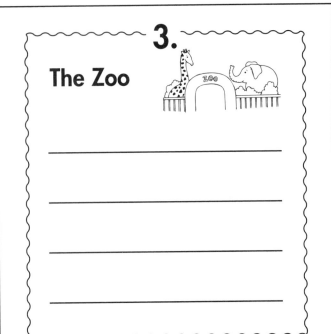

The Zoo

_____

_____

_____

4.

The Carnival

_____

_____

_____

More I'm Through! What Can I Do? Grade 2 © 2008 Creative Teaching Press

Name: _____   Date: _____

Dot-to-Dot Skip Counting

Connect the numbers.

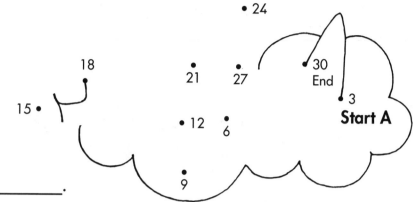

A. I counted by _____.

A. The picture is an _____.

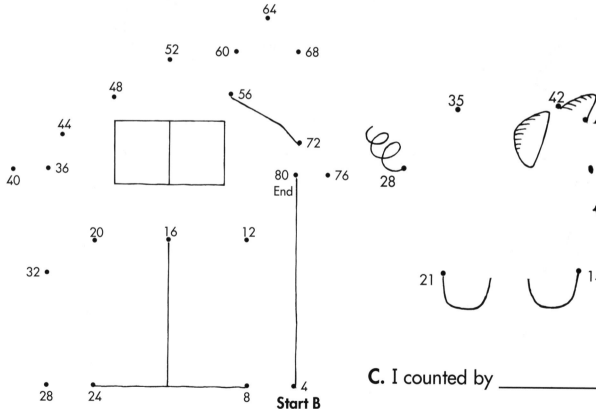

B. I counted by _____.

B. The picture is a _____.

C. I counted by _____.

C. The picture is a _____.

Dot-to-Dot Addition

Add. Then use a crayon to follow the dots in the order of your answers, from 5 to 18.

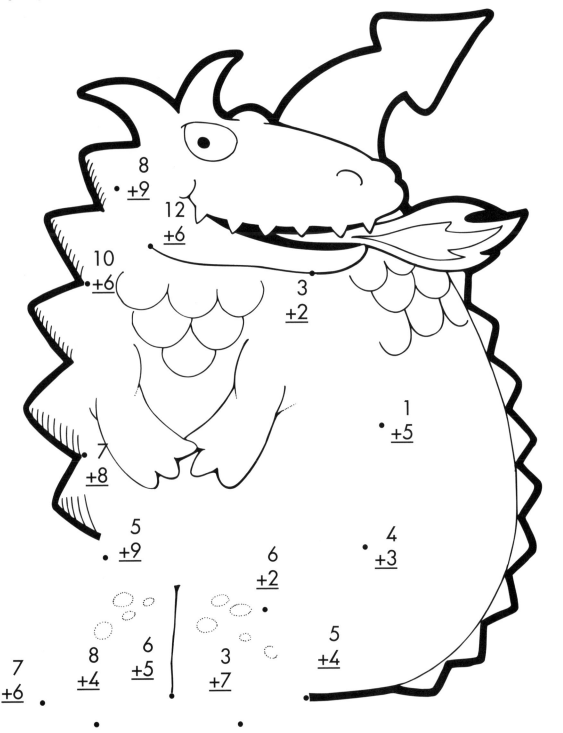

More I'm Through! What Can I Do? Grade 2 © 2008 Creative Teaching Press

Name: _____   Date: _____

Dot-to-Dot Subtraction

Subtract. Then use a crayon to follow the dots in the order of your answers, from 0 to 19.

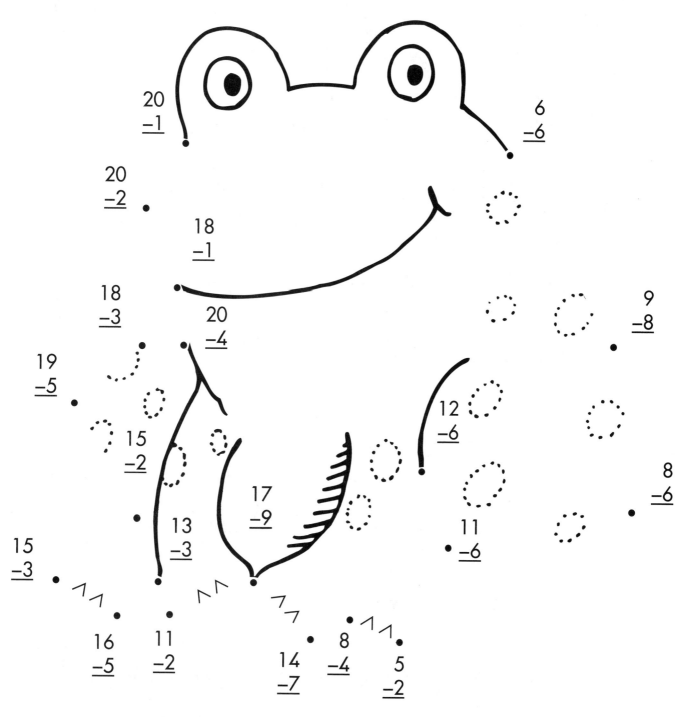

20
−1

6
−6

20
−2

18
−1

18
−3

20
−4

9
−8

19
−5

12
−6

15
−2

8
−6

17
−9

13
−3

11
−6

15
−3

16
−5

11
−2

14
−7

8
−4

5
−2

Number Bubbles

A. Count by twos. Fill in the missing numbers.

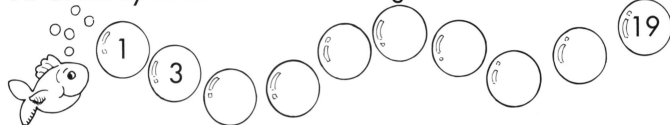

B. Count by fives. Fill in the missing numbers.

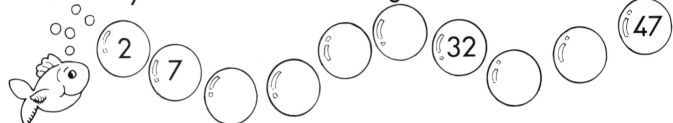

C. Count by tens. Fill in the missing numbers.

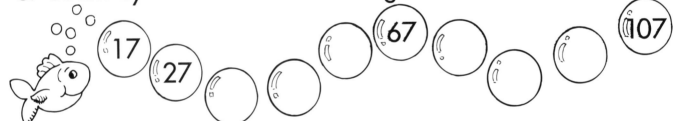

D. Count backwards by tens.

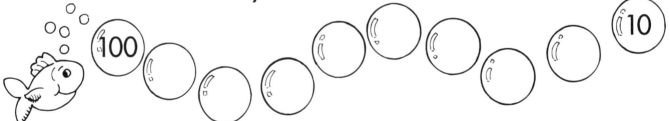

E. Count backwards by fives.

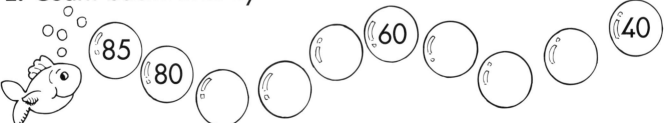

More I'm Through! What Can I Do? Grade 2 © 2008 Creative Teaching Press

Bee to the Hive Maze

Follow the odd numbers to help the bee get to the hive.

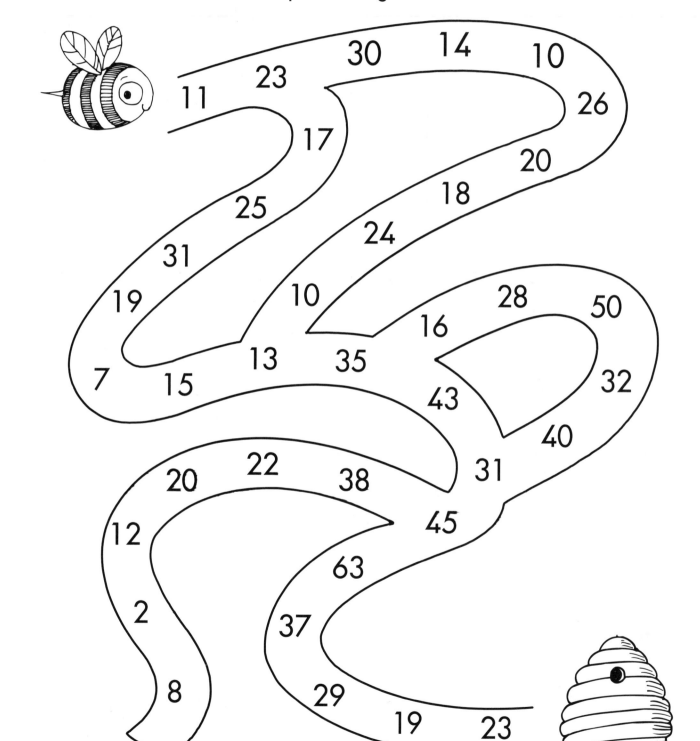

It Equals 10 Maze

Start at the number 10. Move across or down. Color in the boxes that have a sum or difference of 10 to reach the end.

Start

10	$17 - 7$	$4 + 7 + 1$	$14 - 8$	$2 + 9 + 3$
$12 - 4$	$5 + 3 + 2$	$10 + 2 - 2$	$5 + 2 + 3$	$10 - 6 + 2$
$3 + 3 + 6$	$16 - 9$	$4 + 3 + 4$	$18 - 6 - 2$	$4 + 5$
$2 + 2 + 2$	$8 + 6 - 2$	$14 - 3$	$6 + 2 + 2$	$7 + 4$
$8 + 4$	$15 - 6$	$7 + 6$	$13 - 3$	10

Finish

More I'm Through! What Can I Do? Grade 2 © 2008 Creative Teaching Press

Name: ______________________ Date: ____________

Neighborhood Maze

Help Andy take three different paths home. Begin at each arrow and draw the path with a pencil. Then start with 19 and subtract the numbers along each path. Write your answers in the circles.

Name: _____   Date: _____

Cat's Path to 20

Help the cat find its food. Begin at the number under "Start." Find the path of numbers that adds up to 20. End at the number above "End." Write an addition sentence with the numbers you added.

Start

7	6	2	3	2
3	6	5	4	1
2	3	0	8	9
4	0	1	1	0
3	9	4	2	2

End
20

The path of numbers that adds up to 20 is:

_____ .

More I'm Through! What Can I Do? Grade 2 © 2008 Creative Teaching Press

Ant's Path to 0

Help the ant find the food. Begin at the number under "Start." Find the path of numbers that when subtracted equals 0. End at the number above "End." Write a subtraction sentence with the numbers you subtracted.

Start

20	10	5	18	16
9	9	7	3	2
4	6	1	0	6
8	3	4	2	3
5	4	2	1	2

End
0

The path of numbers that when subtracted equals 0 is:

_____ .

Color the Sums—Snowman

Complete the addition problems. Use the key to color the sums.

Key
29–green
37–yellow
48–brown
53–red
65–purple
76–blue
85–white
93–orange

More I'm Through! What Can I Do? Grade 2 © 2008 Creative Teaching Press

Color the Differences—Under the Sea

Subtract. Then color the underwater scene using the differences in the color key.

3 to 4 = **orange**   8 to 10 = **green**   14 to 16 = **yellow**

5 to 7 = **blue**   11 to 13 = **silver**

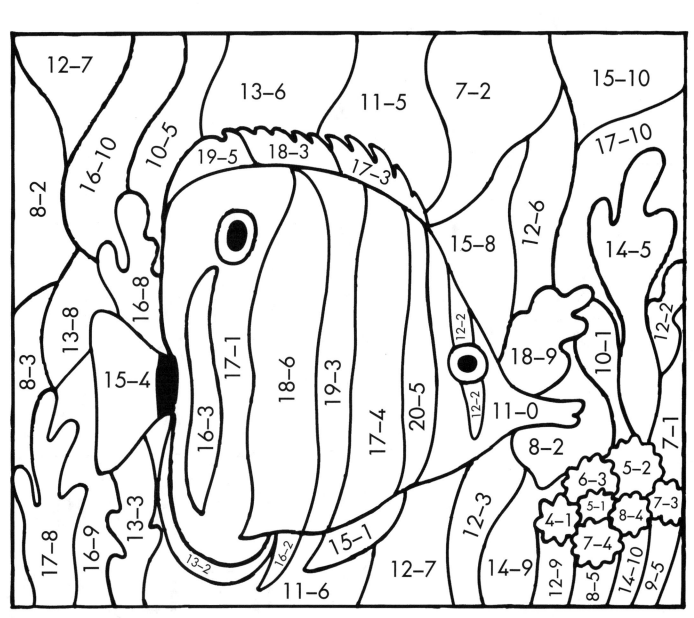

On Target #1

Look at the number in the middle of each target. Next, look at a number in the outside ring. Then decide what number must be added to the middle number to equal the outside number. Write that number in the inside ring. The first one is done for you.

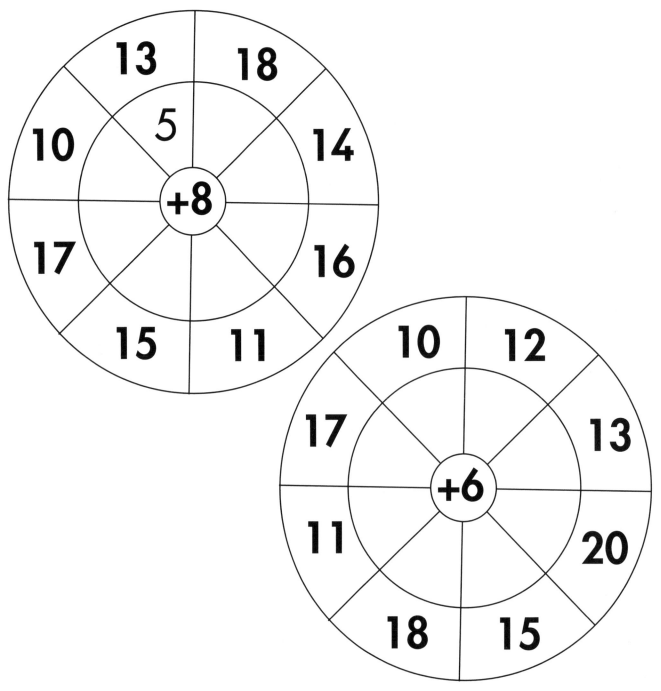

On Target #2

Look at the number in the middle of each target. Next, look at a number in the outside ring. Then decide what number must be added to the middle number to equal the outside number. Write that number in the inside ring. The first one is done for you.

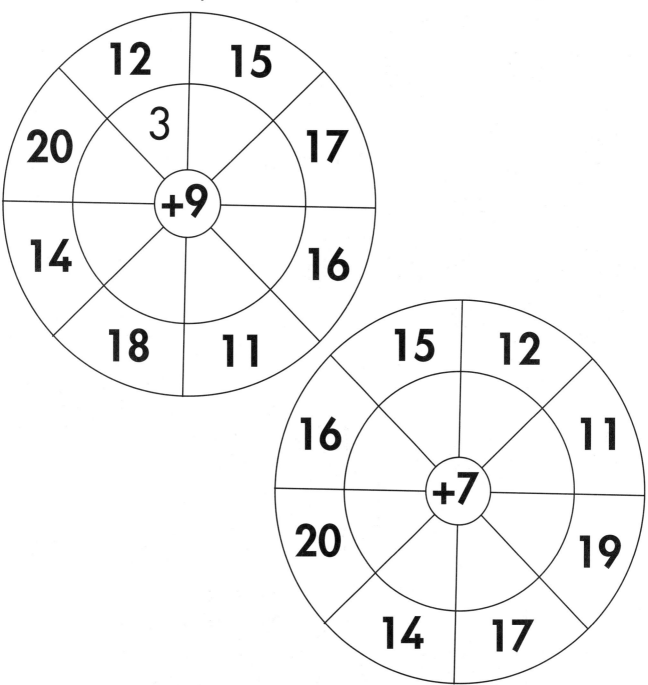

Number Riddles #1

Solve the number riddles. Circle the correct answers.

A. I have 1 ten and 6 ones.
What number am I?

61   16

B. I have 3 tens and 2 ones.
What number am I?

32   23

C. I have 9 ones and less than
4 tens.
What number am I?

49   29

D. I have 2 ones and more than
6 tens.
What number am I?

72   52

E. I have 8 tens and more than
7 ones.
What number am I?

89   86

F. I have 4 tens and less than
5 ones.
What number am I?

47   43

G. I have less than 7 ones and more
than 5 tens.
What number am I?

55   61

H. I have more than 3 ones and less
than 7 tens.
What number am I?

88   56

I. I have less than 5 tens and more
than 4 ones.
What number am I?

54   45

J. I have more than 6 tens and less
than 5 ones.
What number am I?

33   91

More I'm Through! What Can I Do? Grade 2 © 2008 Creative Teaching Press

Number Riddles #2

Solve the number riddles. Circle the correct answers.

A. Both my digits are even. The first digit is smaller than the second digit. The sum of my digits is 10. What number am I?

28   36

B. I am an even number. My second digit is two times my first digit. The sum of my digits is 12. What number am I?

48   24

C. The sum of my digits is an even number. My first digit is six less than my second digit. 12 is the number you get when you add my digits. What number am I?

17   39

D. The sum of my digits is 9. My first digit is larger than my second digit. I am an odd number. What number am I?

63   54

Use similar clues to write your own number riddle in the box below.

Name: _____   Date: _____

Number Riddles #3

Look at the numbers in each bag. Use them to write the numbers that match the clues. Do not use a number in a bag more than once.

A. The number is odd.
  It is greater than 45.
  It is less than 60.

_____

B. The number is even.
  It is greater than 35.
  It is less than 50.

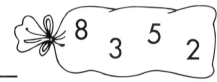

_____

C. The number is even.
  It is greater than 55.
  It is less than 75.

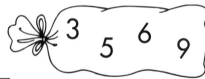

_____

D. The number is odd.
  It is greater than 40.
  It is less than 45.

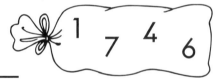

_____

E. The number is even.
  It is greater than 75.
  It is less than 85.

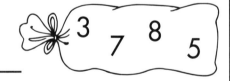

_____

F. The number is odd.
  It is greater than 60.
  It is less than 65.

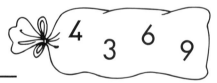

_____

G. The number is odd.
  It is greater than 25.
  It is less than 30.

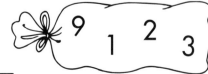

_____

H. The number is even.
  It is greater than 60.
  It is less than 70.

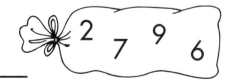

_____

More I'm Through! What Can I Do? Grade 2 © 2008 Creative Teaching Press

Find the Operations

Find the hidden operation symbols. Color them.

Key	
+	plus
−	minus
=	equals
<	less than
>	greater than

A **<** is called a _____ sign. I found ____ of them.

A **+** is called a _____ sign. I found ____ of them.

A **>** is called a _____ sign. I found ____ of them.

A **=** is called an _____ sign. I found ____ of them.

A **−** is called a _____ sign. I found ____ of them.

Name: _____   Date: _____

Subtraction Secret Code— The Donut

Subtract. Write the answers in the boxes under the problems. To find the answer to the riddle, write the letters that match the answers on the lines.

0	1	2	3	4	5	6	7	8	9	10
N	T	I	H	F	E	A	O	L	C	G

Riddle: Why did the donut go to the dentist?

9	14
− 8	− 7

12	9	6
− 2	− 4	− 5

10
− 4

___ ___   ___ ___ ___   ___

17	12	15	16	13	11	12	9	11
− 8	− 9	− 8	− 7	− 6	− 3	− 6	− 8	− 6

___ ___ ___ ___ ___ ___ ___ ___ ___

13	10	14	16	11	10	15
− 9	− 8	− 6	− 8	− 9	− 10	− 5

___ ___ ___ ___ ___ ___ ___ !

More I'm Through! What Can I Do? Grade 2 © 2008 Creative Teaching Press

Addition Secret Code— Rabbit's Riddle

What do you call a rabbit who tells jokes?

To solve the riddle, first answer each problem below.
Then look at your answers and the letters in the boxes.
Look for each answer at the bottom of the page. Then write
the letter from the box above each answer. (You will not use
all the answers and letters.)

f 13 + 5	**b** 66 + 2	**n** 22 + 5	**n** 41 + 7
t 22 + 6	**n** 33 + 5	**y** 65 + 4	**u** 74 + 3
u 70 + 6	**r** 91 + 7	**n** 81 + 4	**y** 56 + 3

A ___ ___ ___ ___ ___   ___ ___ ___ ___ ___ !

18   76   48   38   59   68   77   27   85   69

Hidden Subtraction Problems

There are 13 subtraction problems in this puzzle.
Circle them. They can go **across** or **down**.

Hint: A number can be used in more than one problem.

19	20	20	0	19
2	18	6	12	12
17	3	14	7	7
16	15	1	5	4
11	7	4	2	3

More I'm Through! What Can I Do? Grade 2 © 2008 Creative Teaching Press

Hidden Sums of 50

Find three numbers in a row **across**, **down**, or on a **diagonal** that add up to the sum of 50. Circle each set of three numbers.

22	16	36	23	21	16	30
5	15	21	16	15	29	10
10	14	13	19	23	25	10
15	5	36	17	31	35	25
26	35	18	19	18	17	33
19	10	5	26	19	15	17
32	4	5	14	15	17	9
22	9	19	25	24	14	16
19	6	29	11	3	28	15

I found _____ sums of 50.

Find the Number Sentences

Write **+** or **−** and an **=** between the numbers to make a number sentence. Circle the number sentence. The first one has been done for you.

A. 14 ___ (13 _−_ 7 _=_ 6) ___ 4

B. 5 ___ 6 ___ 11 ___ 2 ___ 8

C. 6 ___ 16 ___ 9 ___ 7 ___ 5

D. 8 ___ 4 ___ 6 ___ 9 ___ 15

E. 8 ___ 9 ___ 17 ___ 10 ___ 6

F. 6 ___ 8 ___ 7 ___ 15 ___ 5

G. 5 ___ 13 ___ 5 ___ 18 ___ 4

H. 4 ___ 6 ___ 20 ___ 12 ___ 8

Make up five more problems like the ones on this page.

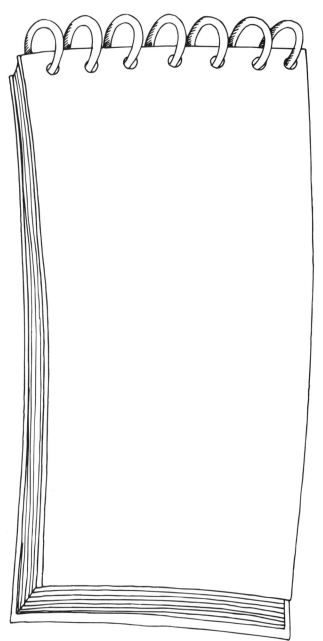

More I'm Through! What Can I Do? Grade 2 © 2008 Creative Teaching Press

What's the Magic Rule? #1

Look at each number going into the magic box and the number coming out of the magic box. What magic rule was used to change the number? Fill in the rest of the missing numbers using the magic rule. Write the rule in the bottom of the box.

Sample Problem

IN	OUT
0	2
8	10
6	**8**
12	**14**
7	**9**
3	**5**
Rule: **+2**	

1.

IN	OUT
12	15
10	13
16	
14	
12	
17	
Rule:	

2.

IN	OUT
20	18
12	10
15	
18	
10	
17	
Rule:	

3.

IN	OUT
10	20
31	41
27	
43	
24	
15	
Rule:	

4.

IN	OUT
5	11
3	7
6	
9	
7	
4	
Rule:	

5.

IN	OUT
15	10
9	4
17	
11	
20	
5	
Rule:	

What's the Magic Rule? #2

Look at each number going into the magic box and the number coming out of the magic box. What magic rule was used to change the number? Fill in the rest of the missing numbers using the magic rule. Write the rule in the bottom of the box.

Sample Problem

IN	OUT
10	11
12	13
14	**15**
16	**17**
18	**19**
20	**21**
Rule: **+1**	

1.

IN	OUT
18	15
12	9
10	
16	
20	
15	
Rule:	

2.

IN	OUT
5	10
6	12
7	
8	
9	
10	
Rule:	

3.

IN	OUT
10	100
2	20
6	
8	
4	
3	
Rule:	

4.

IN	OUT
5	10
12	17
8	
10	
14	
20	
Rule:	

5.

IN	OUT
12	6
10	4
16	
14	
11	
18	
Rule:	

More I'm Through! What Can I Do? Grade 2 © 2008 Creative Teaching Press

What's for Breakfast?

Read the clues. Draw a line to match each food with the correct group of sentences.

1. doughnut

a. I am creamy. You eat me with a spoon. I might have fruit in me.

2. eggs

b. I am a sweet breakfast treat. I have a hole in the middle and frosting on top.

3. cereal

c. You drink me. I am made from fruit.

4. banana

d. You put me in a bowl and eat me with a spoon. You pour milk on me.

5. yogurt

e. You crack me open and cook me in a pan. I am white and yellow.

6. bagel

f. I am thick and round. I taste good with cream cheese.

7. orange juice

g. I am a yellow fruit.

Name: _____   Date: _____

Who's Who?

Read all of the character descriptions. Then decide which description goes best with each picture. Write the name of the characters beneath their pictures.

a. Dad was tired and hot. He was breathing heavily. He said, "That was a hard run but it felt great." Dad always has a good attitude and tries to do his best.

b. She always wore colorful ribbons in her hair and bright-colored clothes. Chelsea liked to talk. She was known as the school "chatterbox." Chelsea Chatterbox to be exact.

c. I used to have a friend named Courtney Cramden, but now I think of her as Crabby Cramden. She always seems to be in a bad mood. She'll find something to complain about, no matter what.

d. Aunt Tina always has a hug and a warm smile for me. She often invites me to stop over for cookies. When we visit, she tells me stories of when she was younger.

1.

_____

2.

_____

3.

_____

4.

_____

Guess Their Ages

Read the clues.
Solve the problems.

A. Kathy is 3 years older than her friend Lisa.

Their ages add up to 13.

How old is Kathy? _____

How old is Lisa? _____

B. Bobby is the same age as his friend Thomas.

In four years, their ages will add up to 20.

How old are they today? _____

C. Melanie's mother is four times as old as Melanie.

When you add their ages together, it adds up to 40.

How old is Melanie? _____

How old is Melanie's mother? _____

D. Annie's father is three times as old as Annie.

Annie's grandfather is two times the age of Annie's father.

The ages of Annie, her father, and her grandfather add up to 100.

How old is Annie? _____

How old is Annie's dad? _____

How old is Annie's grandfather? _____

Pairs of Fish

Mandy's dad said that she can buy two goldfish. The goldfish are red, yellow, and orange. She can buy two fish of the same color or two fish of different colors. Color the fish to show the different pairs Mandy can choose from.

More I'm Through! What Can I Do? Grade 2 © 2008 Creative Teaching Press

Potted Flowers

Mrs. Lane has red, yellow, and purple flowers.
She has green, blue, and brown pots.

Mrs. Lane puts one flower in each pot.
Color the pictures to show the different ways that
Mrs. Lane can mix and match her flowers and pots.

Bear Buddies

There are 6 teddy bears. Each one is a different color.
Read the clues. Find out which bears are together.
Then color the pictures to show how the bears are paired up.

Clues

The brown bear is with either
the yellow bear or the black bear.

The orange bear is with either

the black bear or the purple bear.

The blue bear is with the purple bear.

Odd Word Out

In each row circle the word that does not belong. Then explain on the line below why it does not belong with the other words.

1. lion   frog   dog   bear

   _____

2. stove   bake   boil   fry

   _____

3. robin   salmon   canary   crow

   _____

4. green   blue   orange   crayon

   _____

5. to   three   six   twelve

   _____

6. globe   ball   sun   box

   _____

7. eyes   mouth   leg   ears

   _____

8. day   week   hour   head

   _____

More Odd Word Out

In each row circle the word that does not belong. Then explain on the line below why it does not belong with the other words.

1. lamb   kitten   dog   chick

_____

2. umbrella   rain   snow   wind

_____

3. pine   daisy   rose   tulip

_____

4. zebra   cobra   boa   python

_____

5. milk   juice   steak   tea

_____

6. leaf   banana   lemon   grapes

_____

7. circle   square   triangle   paper

_____

8. aunt   nephew   mother   niece

_____

More I'm Through! What Can I Do? Grade 2 © 2008 Creative Teaching Press

Lucky Coin

Find the lucky coin in the treasure box. Cross out a coin as you find the matching sum in each clue. The lucky coin is the one that is left.

Clues

1. It is not 7 + 5.

2. It is not 13 + 6.

3. It is not 7 + 4.

4. It is not 9 + 9.

5. It is not 5 + 8.

6. It is not 9 + 8.

7. It is not 6 + 4.

8. It is not 6 + 9.

9. It is not 7 + 7

The lucky coin number is _____.

Name: _____   Date: _____

Tonya's Treat

Find Tonya's treat. Read the clues below. Cross out the number below the picture as you read each clue. The number that is left is Tonya's treat!

10   14   5   11

12   2   3

Clues

1. Tonya's treat is not less than 9 − 3.

2. Tonya's treat is not greater than 7 + 6.

3. Tonya's treat is not equal to 14 − 4.

4. Tonya's treat is not an even number.

Tonya's treat is _____.

More I'm Through! What Can I Do? Grade 2 © 2008 Creative Teaching Press

Fun Fit #1

Look at the shape on the left. Turn it around different ways to fit as many as you can on the grid. Color in the shapes as you go. Do not overlap the shapes or place the shapes on shaded squares.

A.

 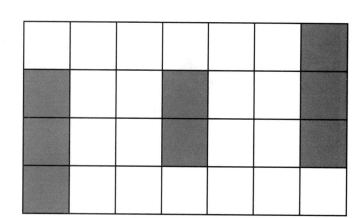

B.

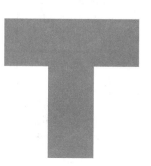 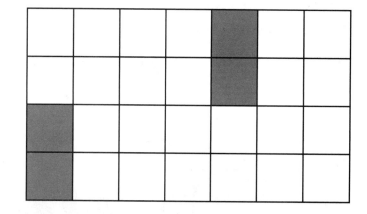

C.

Fun Fit #2

Look at the shape on the left. Turn it around different ways to fit as many as you can on the grid. Color in the shapes as you go. Do not overlap the shapes or place the shapes on shaded squares.

A.

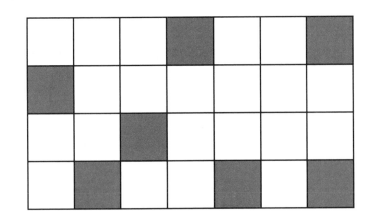

B.

C.

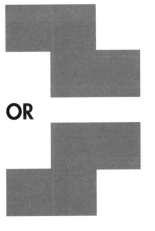

OR

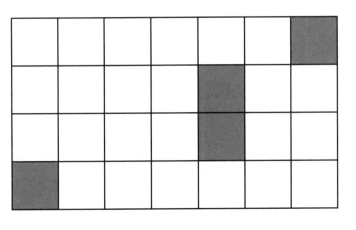

More I'm Through! What Can I Do? Grade 2 © 2008 Creative Teaching Press

Name: _____ Date: _____

Circle Add-Ons

Draw circles to continue each pattern.

A.

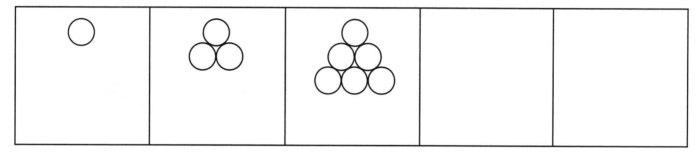

B.

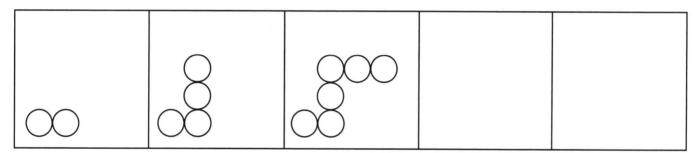

C.

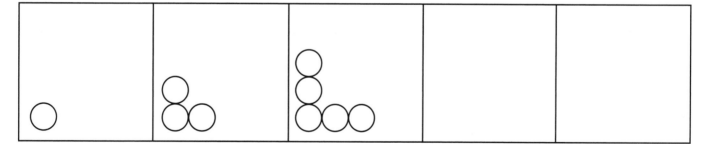

D.

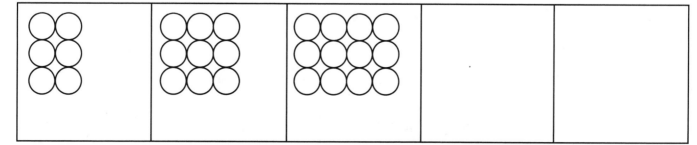

Types of Animals

Follow the directions to mark the pictures of the animals.

1. Color the animal that meows yellow.

2. Underline the animal that slithers.

3. Circle the animal that hops.

4. Draw a box around the animal that lives in the ocean.

5. Color the animal with a long nose green.

6. Draw an X on the animal that lives on a farm.

Animal Opinions

An **opinion** is something that you think or feel. Your opinion may be different than someone else's.

Read the Color Key to the right. Follow the directions and color the animals according to your opinions.

Note: Use only one color for each animal. Not every animal will be colored.

Color Key

Red	your favorite animal
Orange	an animal that is a good pet
Yellow	an animal that is a pest
Green	an animal that is scary
Blue	an animal that everyone loves
Purple	an animal that is friendly

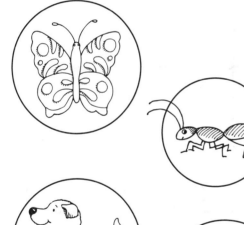

Name: _____   Date: _____

Plant a Crop

Use the key below and follow the directions to plant a crop. Draw your crops.

	1	2	3	4	5	6
A						
B						
C						
D						
E						
F						

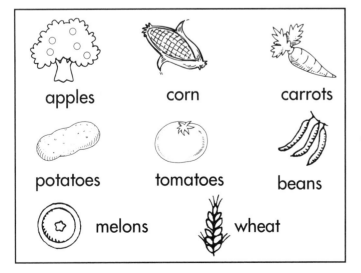

apples   corn   carrots

potatoes   tomatoes   beans

melons   wheat

1. Plant apples in E-5.

2. Plant corn in C-2.

3. Plant tomatoes in C-1 and D-4.

4. Plant melons in A-2.

5. Plant beans in B-6 and D-3.

6. Plant carrots in F-1 and potatoes in F-2.

7. Plant wheat in B-2 and B-3.

More I'm Through! What Can I Do? Grade 2 © 2008 Creative Teaching Press

Build a Zoo

Use the key below and follow the directions to build a zoo. Draw your zoo.

	1	2	3	4	5	6
A						
B						
C						
D						
E						
F						

zoo entrance   bear exhibit   gorilla exhibit

camel exhibit   parking lot   lion exhibit

snack stand   reptile exhibit

1. Place the parking lot in C-1.

2. Place the lion exhibit in C-6.

3. Place the camel exhibit in D-4.

4. Place the zoo entrance in E-2.

5. Place the gorilla exhibit in A-3.

6. Place the bear exhibit in F-3.

7. Place the snack stand in E-5.

8. Place the reptile exhibit in B-4.

Hidden Picture

Follow the directions to see what is hiding. Write your answer below.
1. Color the spaces with odd numbers blue.
2. Color the spaces with even numbers orange.

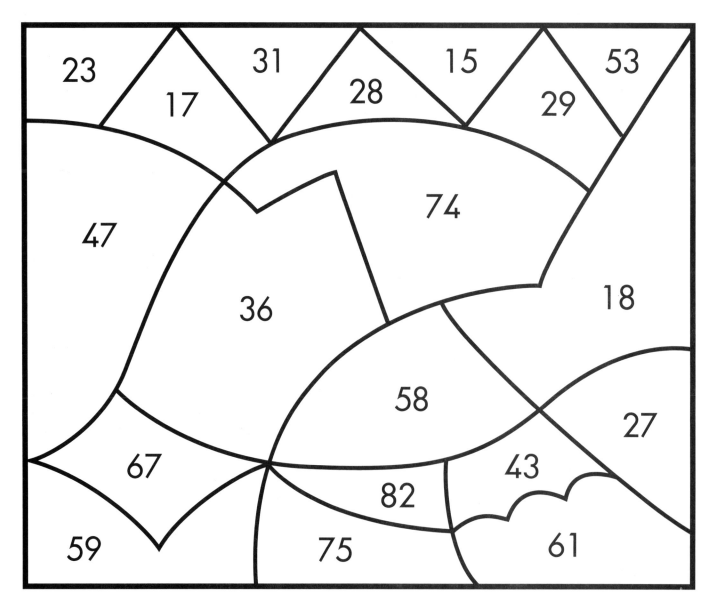

What did you find? _____

More I'm Through! What Can I Do? Grade 2 © 2008 Creative Teaching Press

Name: _____ Date: _____

Birthday Fun

Follow the directions to reveal the secret question. Then answer the question.

1. Cross out all the number words.
2. Cross out all the words that begin with the letter l.
3. Cross out all the color words.

 is

 purple   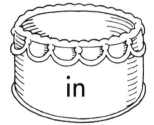 in    twenty    What

 eleven    month    your    little

 birthday    like    fourteen   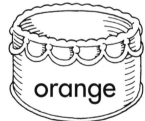 orange

Now unscramble the remaining words and write the question below.

_____

Answer: _____

More I'm Through! What Can I Do? Grade 2 © 2008 Creative Teaching Press

Hidden Message

Follow the directions to reveal the hidden message.

1. Cross out every letter **d**.
2. Cross out every letter **n**.
3. Cross out every letter **p**.
4. Change every **m** to an **s**.
5. Change every **z** to an **f**.

dAnlpwapym   gdinvep

ynopur   bedmtn   deznzonrt!

Now write the letters in order on the lines below to reveal the secret message.

__ __ __ __ __ __ __ __   __ __ __ __ __

__ __ __ __   __ __ __

__ __ __ __ __ __ __!

More I'm Through! What Can I Do? Grade 2 © 2008 Creative Teaching Press

Riddle Fun

Follow the directions to reveal the answer to the riddle.

Why is it dangerous to do math in a jungle?

1. Write the word **you** on line 3 and 8.

2. Write the word **and** on line 6.

3. Write the word **ate** on line 10.

4. Write the word **four** on lines
   5 and 7.

5. Write the word **Because** on line 1.

6. Write the word **if** on line 2.

7. Write the word **add** on line 4.

8. Write the word **get** on line 9.

Answer:

_____   _____   _____   _____   _____
   1   2   3   4   5

_____   _____   _____   _____   _____ **!**
   6   7   8   9   10

Solve the Riddle

What do you call a worm in a fur coat?

Follow the directions below and solve the riddle.

STING	SHIRT	MONKEY	A
TIGER	IT	I'LL	COAT
DON'T	ON	SING	GIRAFFE
AT	BEAR	HAT	IN
ELEPHANT	CAN'T	CATERPILLAR	WING

1. Cross off all the words that rhyme with the word ring.
2. Cross off all the words that have exactly two letters.
3. Cross off all the words that are things people wear.
4. Cross off all the words that are names of zoo animals.
5. Cross off all the words that are contractions.

- Draw a circle around the words that have not been crossed off.
- Start in the top left-hand corner of the puzzle.
- Read the circled words going *across* each row.
- Write the answer to the riddle on the line below.

_____

More I'm Through! What Can I Do? Grade 2 © 2008 Creative Teaching Press

Name: _____   Date: _____

Draw a Beast

Use the pictures and follow the directions to draw your own beast in the box below.

1. Draw a head.

2. Add one giant eye.

3. Give your beast a mouth and a nose.

4. Give your beast curly hair.

5. Add a long body.

6. Give your beast three legs and feet.

7. Give your beast arms and hands.

Treasure Hunt

Use the key to find and color the hidden solid shapes. Write how many of each shape you found.

Key

Color each ⬯ red.

Color each △ yellow.

Color each ⬜ blue.

Color each ⬭ green.

Color each △ orange

I found _____ spheres.

I found _____ pyramids.

I found _____ cubes.

I found _____ cylinders.

I found _____ cones.

Toy Store

Write where each toy can be found in the store. Find the letter and the number that tell which two lines the toy is on. The first one has been done for you.

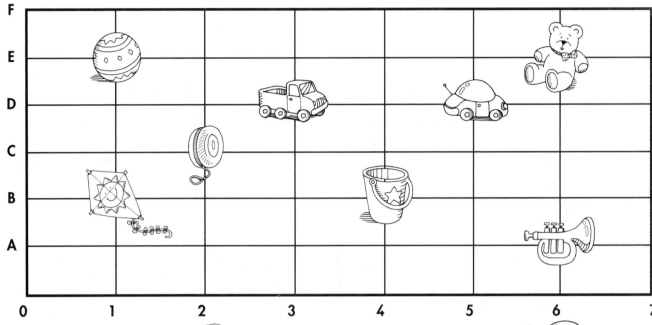

A. Where is the ?

C2

B. Where is the ?

_____

_____

C. Where is the ?

D. Where is the ?

_____

_____

E. Where is the ?

F. Where is the ?

_____

_____

G. Where is the ?

H. Where is the ?

_____

_____

Penguin Maze

Help the penguin get to the igloo. Begin at start.
Find your way through the open path. Do not cross
any solid lines.

Start

Finish

More I'm Through! What Can I Do? Grade 2 © 2008 Creative Teaching Press

Rocket Ship Maze

Help the rocket ship get to outer space. Begin at start. Find your way through the open path. Do not cross any solid lines.

Finish

Start

Worm Maze

Help the worm get to the apple. Begin at start. Find your way through the open path. Do not cross any solid lines.

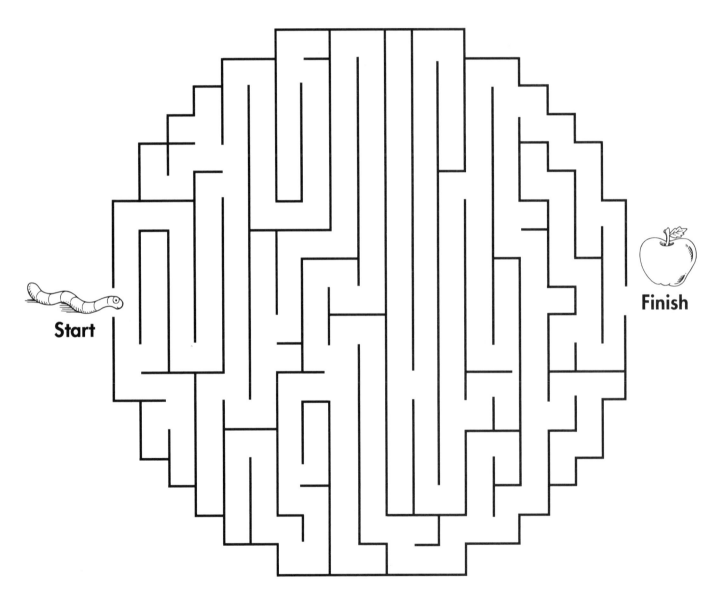

Start

Finish

More I'm Through! What Can I Do? Grade 2 © 2008 Creative Teaching Press

Crack the Code #1

Use the code below to find the answer to the riddle. Write the letter that matches the symbol on each line.

A	B	C	D	E	F	G	H	I	J	K	L	M
●	◄	☯	□	★	☺	◉	&	⬕	Ⅱ	☼	►	✓

N	O	P	Q	R	S	T	U	V	W	X	Y	Z
⚑	👍	🌢	✿	⊠	≈	♈	♓	♦	◇	✦	❀	➤

Riddle: Why didn't anyone want to sleep next to the daddy dinosaur?

Answer:

Crack the Code #2

Use the code below to find the answer to the riddle. Write the letter that matches the symbol on each line.

A	B	C	D	E	F	G	H	I	J	K	L	M
●	◄	☯	□	★	☺	◉	&	⌂	Ⅱ	✿	➤	✓

N	O	P	Q	R	S	T	U	V	W	X	Y	Z
⚑	👍	●	❀	☒	≈	♈	♓	◆	✦	❖	✠	◄

Riddle: What did the flag say to the pole?

Answer:

More I'm Through! What Can I Do? Grade 2 © 2008 Creative Teaching Press

Finish the Picture—Gingerbread Man

Finish the picture by drawing the missing half. Make the right side symmetrical to the left side. Color the picture when you are finished.

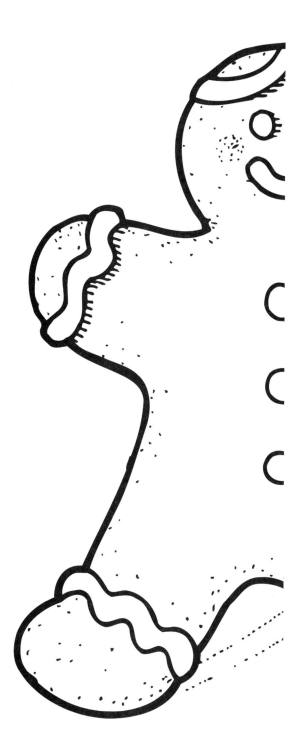

Finish the Picture—Winter Sweater

Finish the picture by drawing the missing half. Make the right side symmetrical to the left side. Color the picture when you are finished.

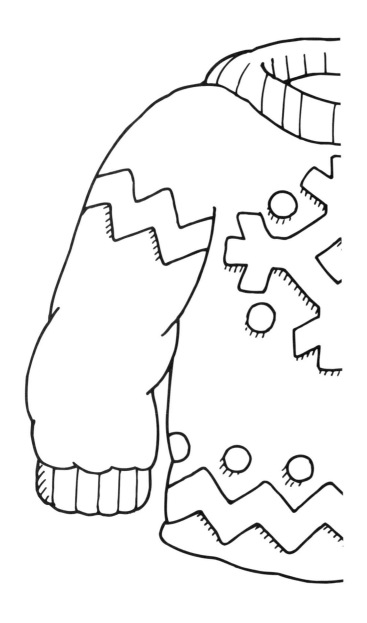

More I'm Through! What Can I Do? Grade 2 © 2008 Creative Teaching Press

Finish the Picture—King's Castle

Finish the picture by drawing the missing half. Make the right side symmetrical to the left side. Color the picture when you are finished.

Answer Key

Three-in-a-Row—Long *O* (page 5)

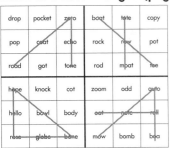

drop	pocket	zero	boat	tote	copy
pop	coat	echo	rock	row	pot
road	got	tone	rod	moat	toe
hope	knock	cot	zoom	odd	auto
hello	bowl	body	oat	note	roll
rose	globe	bone	mow	bomb	boa

Three-in-a-Row—Two Syllable Words (page 6)

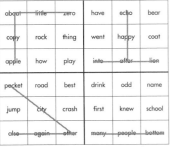

about	little	zero	have	echo	bear
copy	rock	thing	went	happy	coat
apple	how	play	into	offer	lion
pocket	road	best	drink	odd	name
jump	city	crash	first	knew	school
also	again	other	many	people	bottom

Three-in-a-Row—Nouns (page 7)

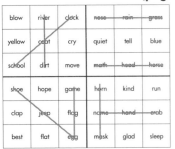

blow	river	clock	nose	rain	grass
yellow	coat	cry	quiet	tell	blue
school	dirt	move	math	head	horse
shoe	hope	game	horn	kind	run
clap	jeep	flag	name	hand	crab
best	flat	egg	mask	glad	sleep

Find the Rhyme #1 (page 8)

Find the Rhyme #2 (page 9)

1. sweet
2. train
3. globe
4. spring
5. snake
6. flash
7. frog
8. throw
9. cry
10. stretch

Find the Hidden Picture—Hard and Soft *c* and *g* (page 10)

Answers will vary.

Find the Hidden Picture—How Many Syllables? (page 11)

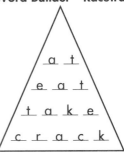

I see a frog.

Find Your Way—Words with *str* (page 12)

street	strike	stran
strime	string	strice
stred	stream	strish
strame	stripe	strap
streed	stren	strain

Find Your Way—ABC Order (page 13)

again	because	bath
first	boat	help
gave	grip	kind
goes	made	mine
open	most	pull

Find Your Way—Action Words (page 14)

skip	boat	pretty
look	swim	top
nice	buy	tree
pen	jump	give
dime	oven	sing

Word Builder—Friend (page 15)

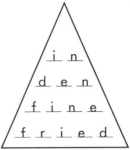

Answers will vary.

Word Builder—Birthday (page 16)

Answers will vary.

Word Builder—Racetrack (page 17)

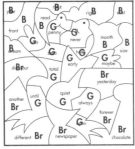

Answers will vary.

Word Scramble—Mystery Long *e* Sound (page 18)

1. knee or keen
2. treat
3. wheel
4. street
5. sheep
6. sweet
7. city
8. meet
9. baby
10. real

Answer: The mystery letter is y!

Word Scramble—R-Controlled Vowels (page 19)

1. dirt
2. first
3. horn
4. turtle
5. finger
6. dart
7. her
8. car
9. hurt
10. bird

Answer: The letter r!

Word Scramble—Fruits and Vegetables (page 20)

1. orange
2. banana
3. beans
4. apple
5. radish
6. broccoli
7. kiwi
8. carrot
9. celery
10. grapes

Answer: I don't peel very well.

Magic Word Square #1 (page 21)

Possible answers include:

hop	mow
bop	who
low	soy
bow	plow
how	slob
boy	slop
mob	slow
mop	

Magic Word Square #2 (page 22)

Possible answers include:

any	yap
lap	only
lay	pale
nap	plan
pal	play
pan	loyal
pay	pylon

Compound Crossword (page 23)

Across:
1. anthill
2. horsefly
5. starfish
6. teapot
7. playpen

Down:
1. airplane
3. lighthouse
4. baseball

Same or Opposite? Crossword (page 24)

Across:
2. kind
7. first
8. buy
9. imitate
10. sweet

Down:
1. gather
3. damp
4. hot
5. light
6. full

Human Body Word Search (page 25)

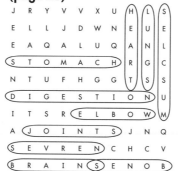

Types of Animals Word Search (page 26)

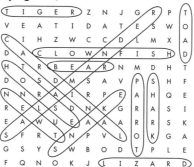

Landforms and Bodies of Water Word Search (page 27)

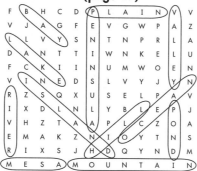

Fun with Words #1 (page 28)

Possible answers include:

Fruit: grape, raspberry, orange, watermelon

Animal: giraffe, rat, otter, weasel

Place: garden, ranch, Ohio, Washington

Name: George, Ruth, Olivia, Wendy

Fun with Words #2 (page 29)

Possible answers include:

A: ant, Adam, arm, anthill

C: car, correct, crib, cupcake

M: mat, music, mother, moonlight

O: oat, organ, octopus, oatmeal

W: went, window, wagon, without

The Five Senses (page 30)

Hear: sizzle, shhh, pop, buzz, crackle

Feel: hard, smooth, bumpy, ridged

Taste: sweet, sour, bitter, salty, spicy

Smell: stinky, cinnamon, rotten

See: black, huge, pink, tiny, bright, square, thin, giant, tall

Adding Details (page 31)

1. along the rocky path.
2. for her doctor.
3. in the yard.
4. late for work.
5. yesterday after school.
6. in the cold lake.

Main Idea and Details—All About Families (page 32)

The children who are saying the following sentences should be colored.

My family eats meals together.

My mom and I enjoy playing games.

My sister and I ride bikes after school.

After dinner we help each other clean up.

What's the Main Idea? (page 33)

1. fruits
2. animals
3. feelings or emotions
4. shapes

Main Idea and Details—A Day of Fun (page 34)

Possible answers include:

1. swim, build a sandcastle, collect shells
2. swing, play in the sand, climb the monkey bars
3. feed the seals, watch the monkeys, buy a souvenir
4. ride the Ferris wheel, eat cotton candy, win a prize

Dot-to-Dot Skip Counting (page 35)

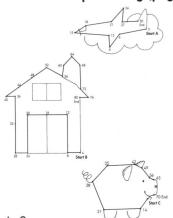

A. 3s

A. airplane

B. 4s

B. barn

C. 7s

C. pig

Dot-to-Dot Addition (page 36)

Dot-to-Dot Subtraction (page 37)

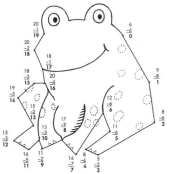

Number Bubbles (page 38)

A. 1, 3, **5, 7, 9, 11, 13, 15, 17,**19

B. 2, 7, **12, 17, 22, 27,** 32, **37, 42,** 47

C. 17, 27, **37, 47, 57,** 67, **77, 87, 97,** 107

D. 100, **90, 80, 70, 60,** 50, **40, 30, 20,** 10

E. 85, 80, **75, 70, 65,** 60, **55, 50, 45,** 40

Bee to the Hive Maze (page 39)

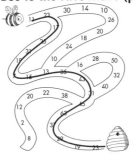

It Equals 10 Maze (page 40)

10	17−7	4+7+1	14−8	2+9+3
12−4	5+3+2	10+2−2	5+2+3	10−6+2
3+3+6	16−9	4+3+4	16−6−2	4+5
2+2+2	8+6−2	14−3	6+2+2	7+4
8+4	15−6	7+6	13−3	10

Neighborhood Maze (page 41)

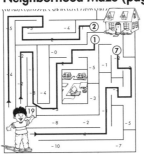

Cat's Path to 20 (page 42)

7	6	2	3	2
3	6	5	4	1
2	3	0	8	9
4	0	1	1	0
3	9	4	2	2

Ant's Path to 0 (page 43)

20	10	5	18	16
9	9	7	3	2
4	6	1	0	6
8	3	4	2	3
5	4	2	1	2

Color the Sums—Snowman (page 44)

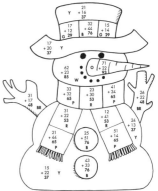

Color the Differences—Under the Sea (page 45)

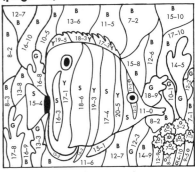

On Target #1 (page 46)

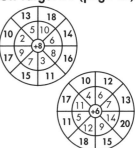

On Target #2 (page 47)

Number Riddles #1 (page 48)

A. 16   B. 32

C. 29   D. 72

E. 89   F. 43

G. 61   H. 56

I. 45   J. 91

Number Riddles #2 (page 49)

A. 28   C. 39

B. 48   D. 63

Number Riddles #3 (page 50)

A. 47   B. 38

C. 56   D. 41

E. 78   F. 63

G. 29   H. 62

Find the Operations (page 51)

/less than/8

/plus/10

/greater than/4

/equals/11

/minus/8

Subtraction Secret Code—The Donut (page 52)

Answer to riddle: To get a chocolate filling!

Addition Secret Code—Rabbit's Riddle (page 53)

Row 1: 18, 68, 27, 48

Row 2: 28, 38, 69, 77

Row 3: 76, 98, 85, 59

Answer to riddle: A funny bunny!

Hidden Subtraction Problems (page 54)

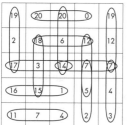

Hidden Sums of 50 (page 55)

Find the Number Sentences (page 56)

A. 14 (13 − 7 = 6) 4

B. (5 + 6 = 11) 2 8

C. 6 (16 − 9 = 7) 5

D. 8 3 (6 + 9 = 15)

E. (8 + 9 = 17) 10 6

F. 6 (8 + 7 = 15) 5

G. 5 (13 + 5 = 18) 4

H. 4 6 (20 − 12 = 8)

What's the Magic Rule? #1 (page 57)

1. Out: 15, 13, **19, 17, 15, 20**
   Rule: **+ 3**

2. Out: 18, 10, **13, 16, 8, 15**
   Rule: **− 2**

3. Out: 20, 41, **37, 53, 34, 25**
   Rule **+ 10**

4. Out: 11, 7, **13, 19, 15, 9**
   Rule: doubles **+1**

5. Out: 10, 4, **12, 6, 15, 0**
   Rule: **− 5**

What's the Magic Rule? #2 (page 58)

1. Out: 15, 9, **7, 13, 17, 12**
   Rule: **− 3**

2. Out: 10, 12, **14, 16, 18, 20**
   Rule: **x 2**

3. Out: 100, 20, **60, 80, 40, 30**
   Rule **x 10**

4. Out: 10, 17, **13, 15, 19, 25**
   Rule: **+ 5**

5. Out: 6, 4, **10, 8, 5, 12**
   Rule: **− 6**

What's for Breakfast? (page 59)

1. b

2. e

3. d

4. g

5. a

6. f

7. c

Who's Who? (page 60)

1. d; Aunt Tina

2. c; Courtney

3. a; Dad

4. b; Chelsea

Guess Their Ages (page 61)

A. Kathy is 8, Lisa is 5.

B. 6

C. Melanie is 8, Melanie's mother is 32.

D. Annie is 10, Annie's father is 30, Annie's grandfather is 60.

Pairs of Fish (page 62)

Fish should be colored to show these combinations: red and red, red and yellow, red and orange, yellow and yellow, yellow and orange, orange and orange.

Potted Flowers (page 63)

Flowers and pots should be colored to show these combinations: red flower/green pot; red flower/blue pot; red flower/brown pot; yellow flower/green pot; yellow flower/blue pot; yellow flower/brown pot; purple flower/green pot; purple flower/blue pot; purple flower/brown pot.

Bear Buddies (page 64)

Bears should be colored to show these combinations: blue and purple, orange and black, brown and yellow. Tip: It may be helpful for students to manipulate colored squares (blue, purple, orange, black, brown, yellow) in order to solve the problem.

Odd Word Out (page 65)

1. frog—not a mammal

2. stove—not a way to cook food

3. salmon—not the name of a bird

4. crayon—not the name of a color

5. to—not the name of a number

6. box—not an object that is round

7. leg—not a part of the head or face

8. head—not a measurement of time

More Odd Word Out (page 66)

1. dog—not the name of a baby animal

2. umbrella—not a type of weather

3. pine—not the name of a flower

4. zebra—not the name of a snake

5. steak—not something you drink; not a liquid

6. leaf—not a fruit

7. paper—not the name of a geometric shape

8. nephew—not a female relative

Lucky Coin (page 67)

The lucky coin number is **16**.

Tonya's Treat (page 68)

Tonya's treat is the **pie**.

Fun Fit #1 (page 69)

Possible answers include:

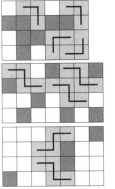

Fun Fit #2 (page 70)

Possible answers include:

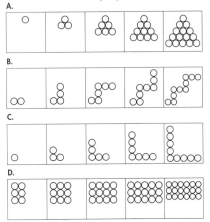

Circle Add-Ons (page 71)

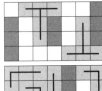

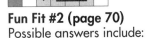

Types of Animals (page 72)

1. cat
2. snake
3. frog
4. whale
5. alligator
6. rooster

Animal Opinions (page 73)

Answers will vary.

Plant a Crop (page 74)

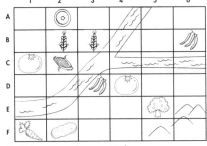

Build a Zoo (page 75)

Hidden Picture (page 76)

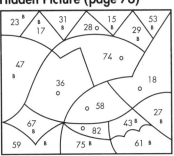

A fish.

Birthday Fun (page 77)

What month is your birthday in?

Hidden Message (page 78)

Always give your best effort!

Riddle Fun (page 79)

Because if you add four and four you get ate!

Solve the Riddle (page 80)

A caterpillar.

Draw a Beast (page 81)

Pictures will vary.

Treasure Hunt (page 82)

I found **8** spheres. I found **6** cylinders.
I found **4** pyramids. I found **3** cones.
I found **5** cubes.

Toy Store (page 83)

A. C2
B. D5
C. E1
D. B1
E. A6
F. E6
G. D3
H. B4

Penguin Maze (page 84)

Rocket Ship Maze (page 85)

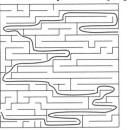

Worm Maze (page 86)

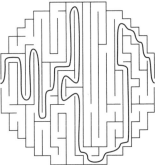

Crack the Code #1 (page 87)

Because he was a bronto-snore-us!

Crack the Code #2 (page 88)

It didn't say anything. It just waved!

Finish the Picture—Gingerbread Man (page 89)

Drawing should be symmetrical.

Finish the Picture—Winter Sweater (page 90)

Drawing should be symmetrical.

Finish the Picture—King's Castle (page 91)

Drawing should be symmetrical.